Name_____

My Prayer
Coloring Book

XULON PRESS

My Prayer Coloring Book
By: Mom Mary B. Campbell
Of Mary's Heart, LLC.
Copyright 2007

Illustrated By:
Jeri Treadwell

ENDORSEMENTS

Thanks Mary for the gift this coloring book will be to children, our city, state and nation when others catch the idea. Even older people are coloring these days. What a wonderful and unique idea to get the little ones' minds set on God before they are filled with the world's clutter. Let coloring begin! ~ Mim Stern

The approach is refreshing, enlightening and entertaining for young children just learning about relationships and the role as children of God.
I have been working with Christian education and Mary Campbell in the National Day of Prayer and my Promise Keepers for the past 12 years thus; I wholeheartedly endorse this prayer coloring book for children ages Pre-K to 5 in every culture and at every income level to draw them closer to God and preferably interceding for everyone they know! ~ Rev. John W. Mosley, Jr.

Do you want to see America transformed? If every child learns how to pray from Mother Mary Campbell, it will be! A wonderful mother and a powerful intercessor, Mary focuses the children and their prayers on what is truly important. ~ Ted Hewson

Thanks for sharing this with me, Mary. The coloring book looks fun, engaging, Christ honoring and exquisite with color. May God use it to honor His name, and introduce others to the Savior.
~ Ron Walters, Senior V.P. of National Ministries, Salem Media Group

Mary Campbell knows what it is to be in the presence of "Almighty God" and knows how to bring God's presence into the lives of others.
This little book can actually build "world changers" because it will bring them into the presence that created the entire universe. This book will change lives for the glory of God. ~ Jim Maxim, Founder of Acts 413 Ministries

Mary Campbell is a widely recognized and respected prayer leader in the Greater Philadelphia region. Many see her as a spiritual mother whose passion for a work of God that touches the generations is contagious. Mary truly inspires others to faithfulness to the call of God, and faith in the power of God to transform our nation. ~ Ed Crenshaw, Victory Church Philadelphia

We thank God for "My Prayer Coloring Book". We believe that a part of God's assignment in the publishing of this book is to "Prepare the Way of the Lord in the Heart of a Child". The fruit of this book is a testimony of Mary Campbell's faithfulness in His vineyard. Children are His treasure!
~ Apostle Phillip & Carolyn Heflin

Day Care Center teachers can easily integrate My Prayer Coloring Book into the book collection. Children will have fun and learn how to pray while coloring the pages. ~ Yvonne M. Florence, Prayer Advocate for Day Care Ctrs

Strategic, intentional, transformational prayer is what we need in our lives and in our nation! Mary Campbell, a true leader and a mother in the prayer movement, has created a simple but powerful coloring book that will engage, equip, and encourage children to pray for our nation, one center of influence at a time! I highly recommend it! ~ Dion Elmore, Chief Communications Officer, National Day of Prayer Task Force

Mary Campbell has a heart for God, for prayer, and for people.
I have never known a greater exemplification of a "prayer warrior" than Mary Campbell. Not only does she make it her priority to personally mediate between God and His children, she also encourages others to pray as one of the great leaders of prayer in Philadelphia and Pennsylvania. Mary founded the Prayer in the City movement—an event in which I have participated on multiple occasions—where believers from a variety of backgrounds come together to pray for the City of Philadelphia. In addition, she was honored by the National Day of Prayer Task Force at the White House, and she was acknowledged with a citation from Mayor Nutter for her outstanding work in Philadelphia through the National Day of Prayer. Mary's list of achievements in the battleground of prayer ministry is indeed remarkable. I am proud that my name is on her lips, because there is no doubt that Mary Campbell is a righteous person. And we know that, according to James 5:16b, "The prayer of a righteous person is powerful and effective."
~ Rev. Bonnie Camarda, Dir. of Partnerships, The Salvation Army

Mary's Heart, LLC

www.xulonpress.com

With Gratitude

First, thanks be to Almighty God, our Father, for the idea of the project, for we know that all good gifts come from above. James 1:17

Thanks to my daughter Ursula C. Simmons who partnered
With leaders of Christian Day Care Centers to promote the project

Thanks to my Senior minister Dr. James David Treadwell, Jr. for his blessings

Thanks to my employers; Russ Whitnah and Carol Healey who introduced the project to Salem Media Group and Xulon Press

Thanks to all who have taken part in any way to make this a reality
(prayer, encouragement, physical and financial support)

To God be the Glory
Mary B. Campbell

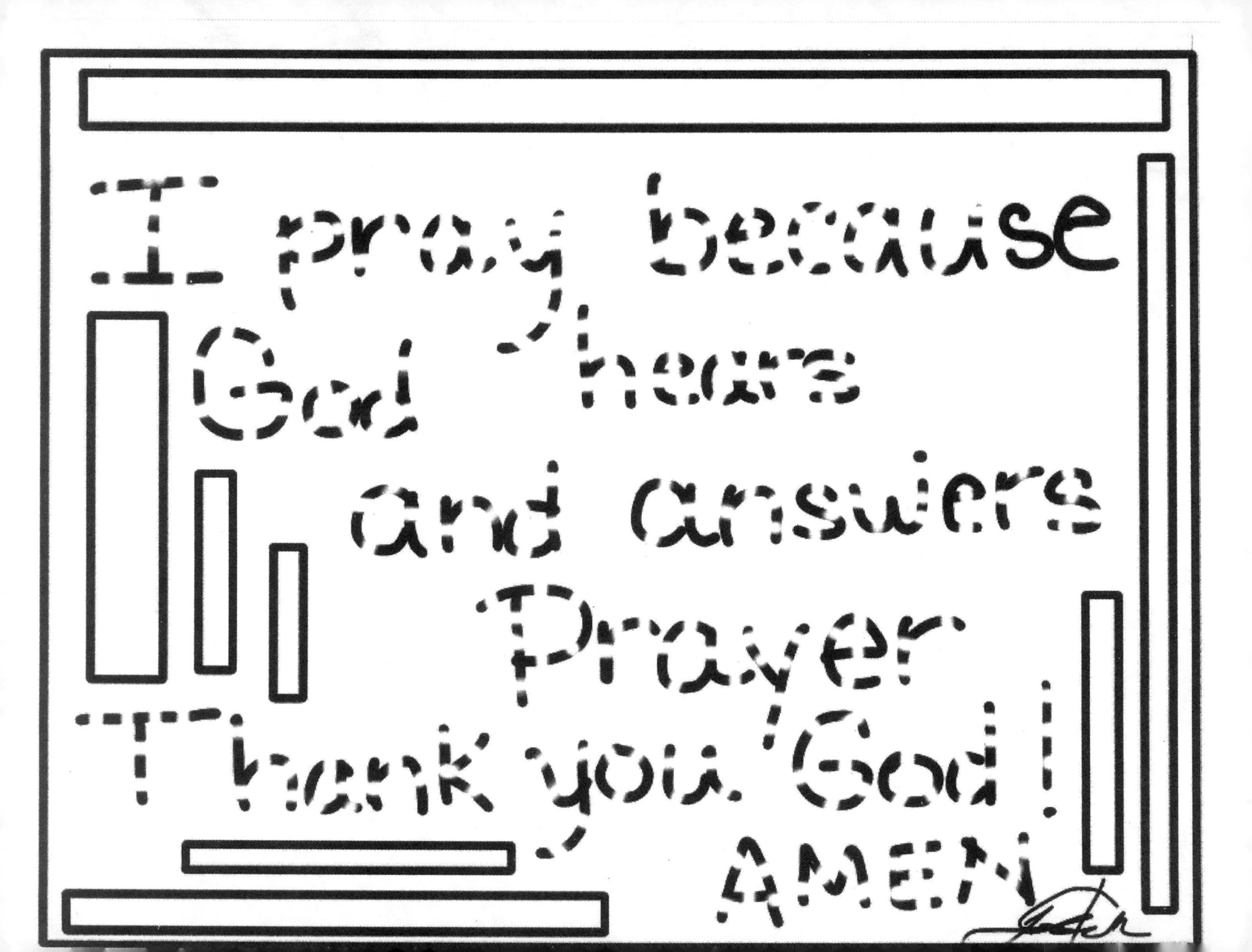

I Pray for My family

I PRAY FOR MY FAMILY AND OTHER FAMILIES

I pray for my Education

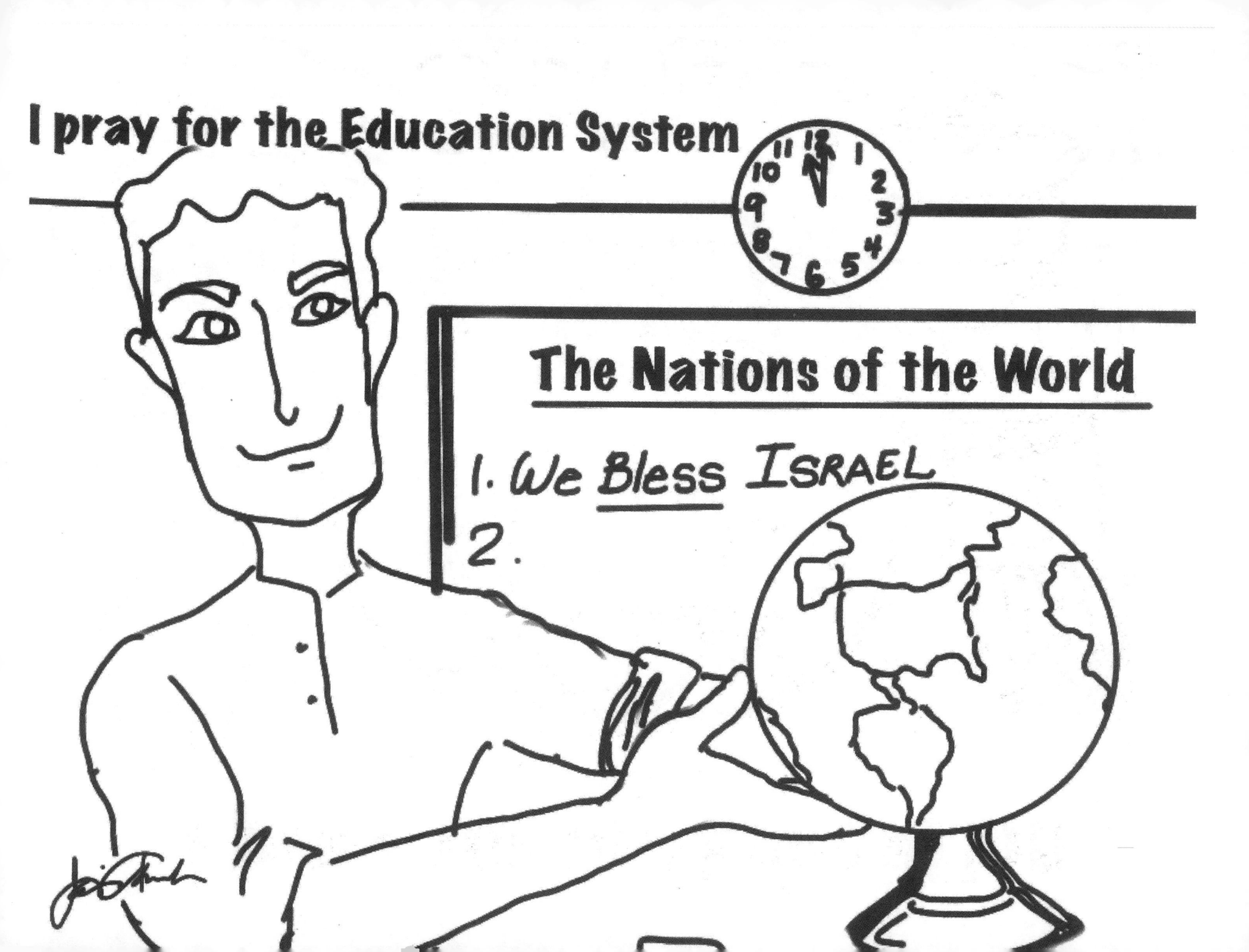

I Pray for my School and all other Schools.

I Pray for the Schools

I Pray for My Teacher

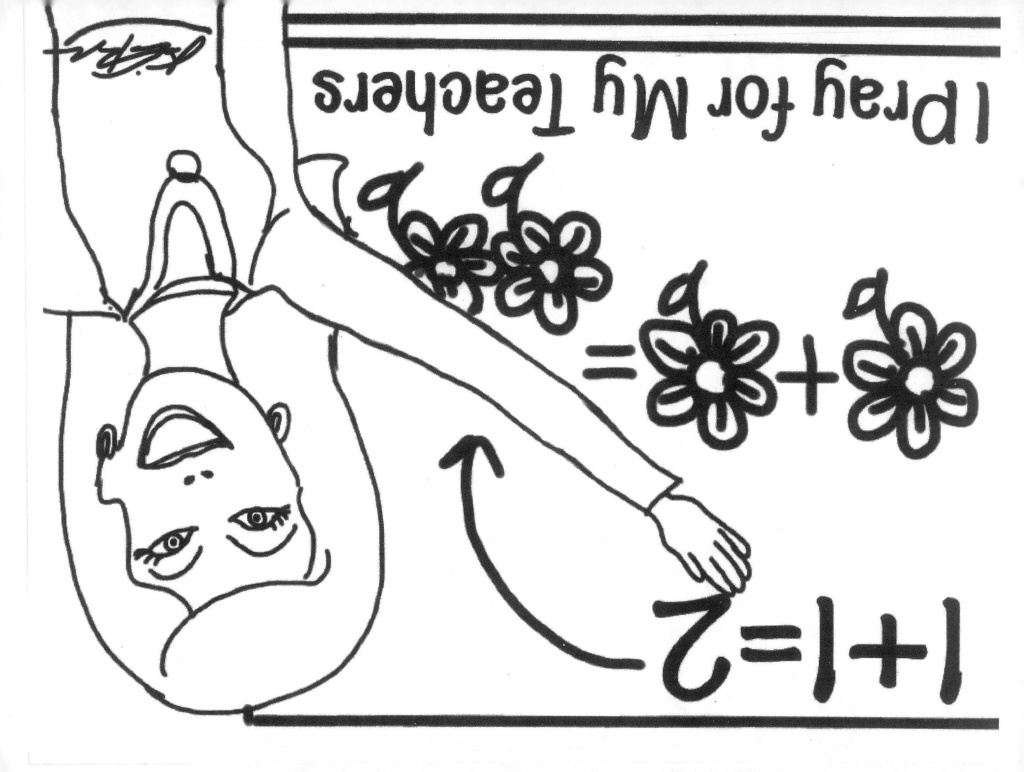

I Love to Pray

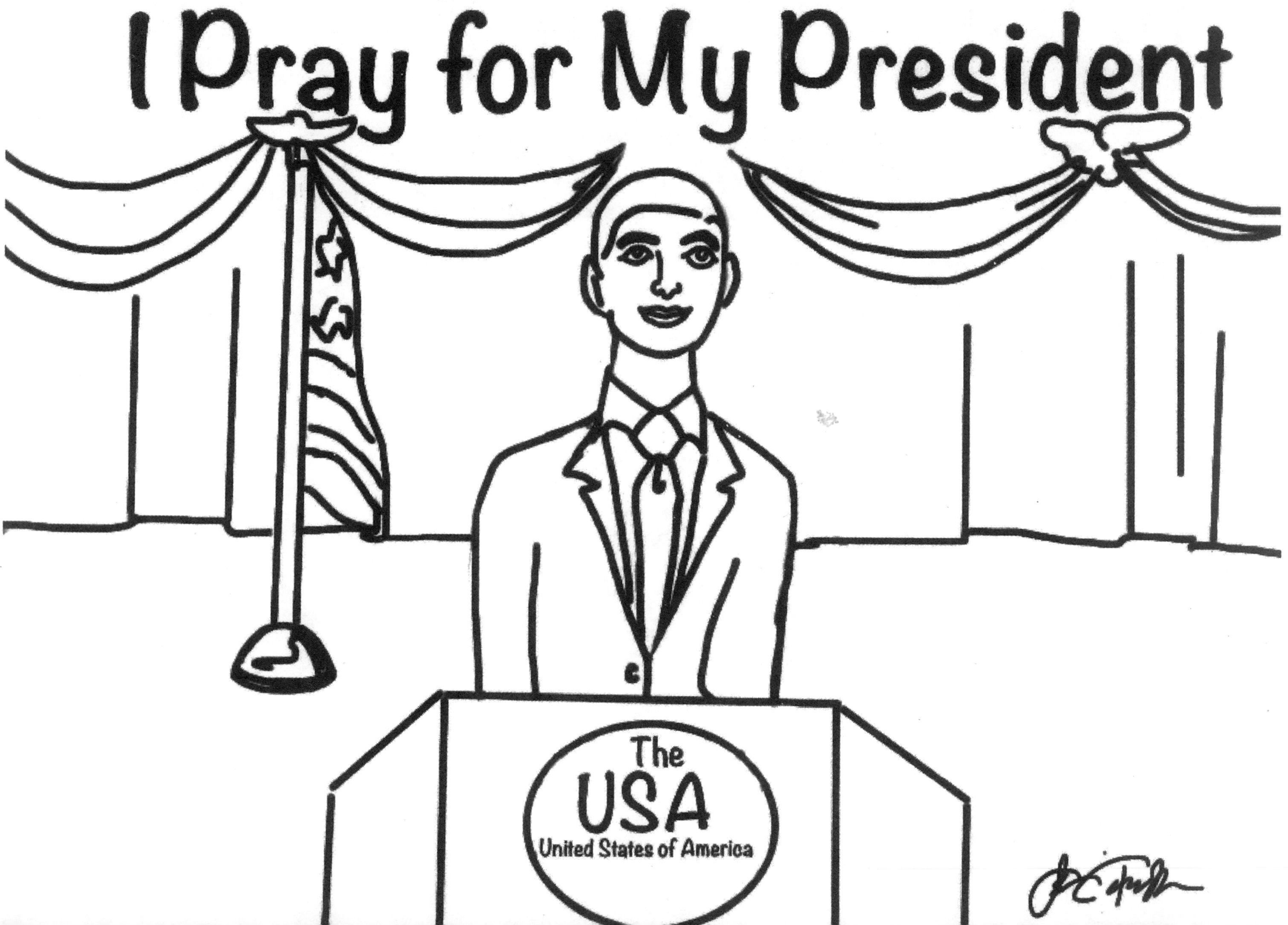
I Pray for My President
The
USA
United States of America

I Pray for my Church

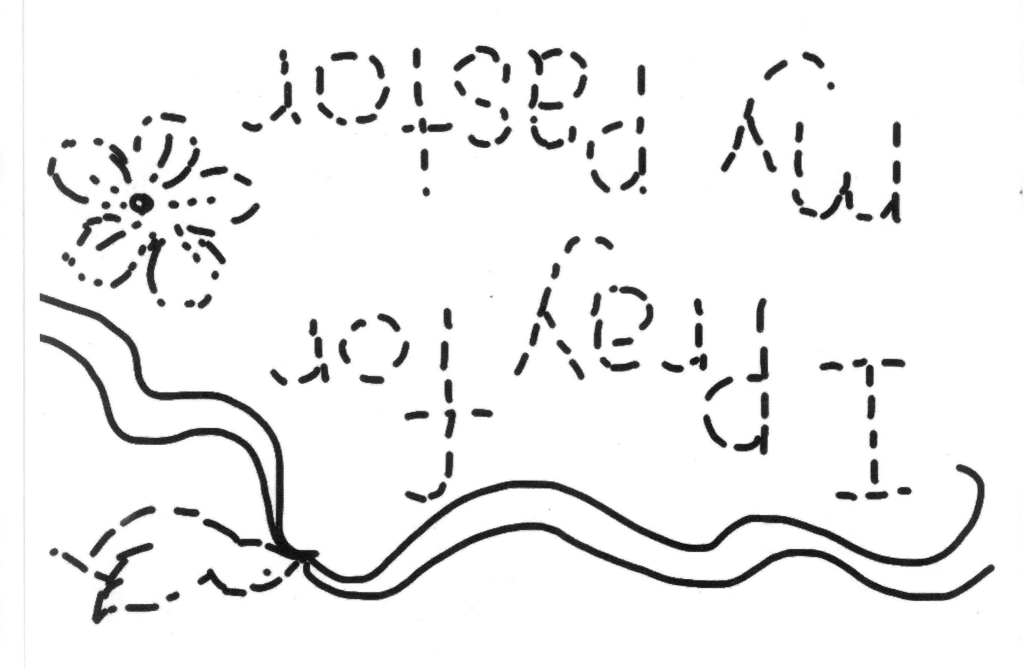

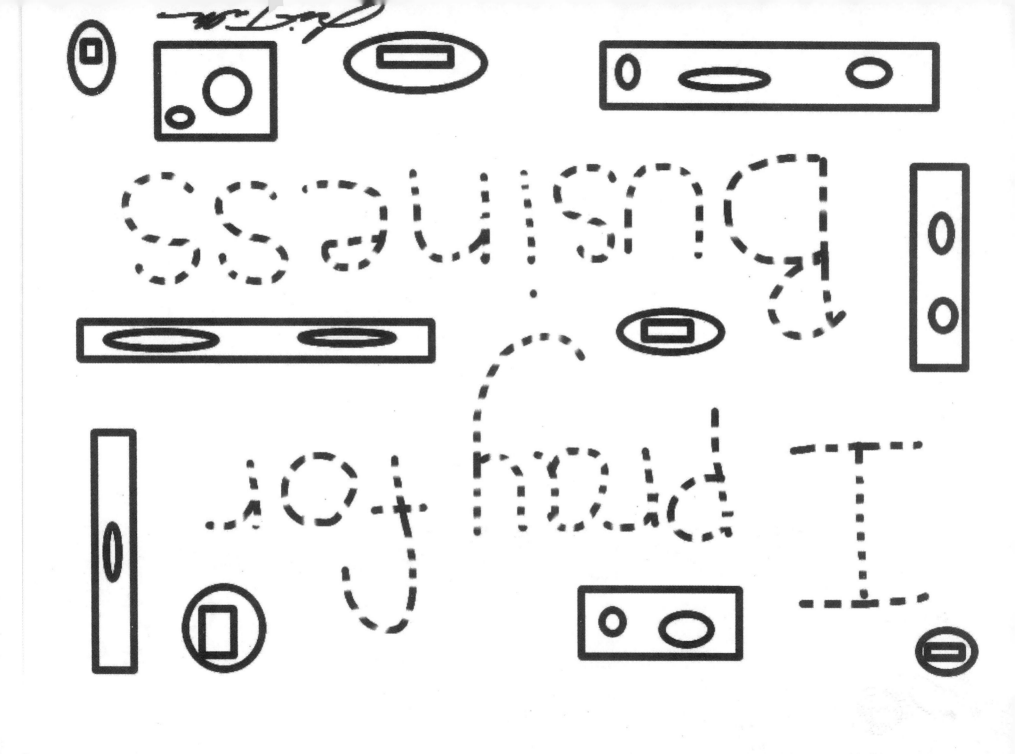

I pray for the Media

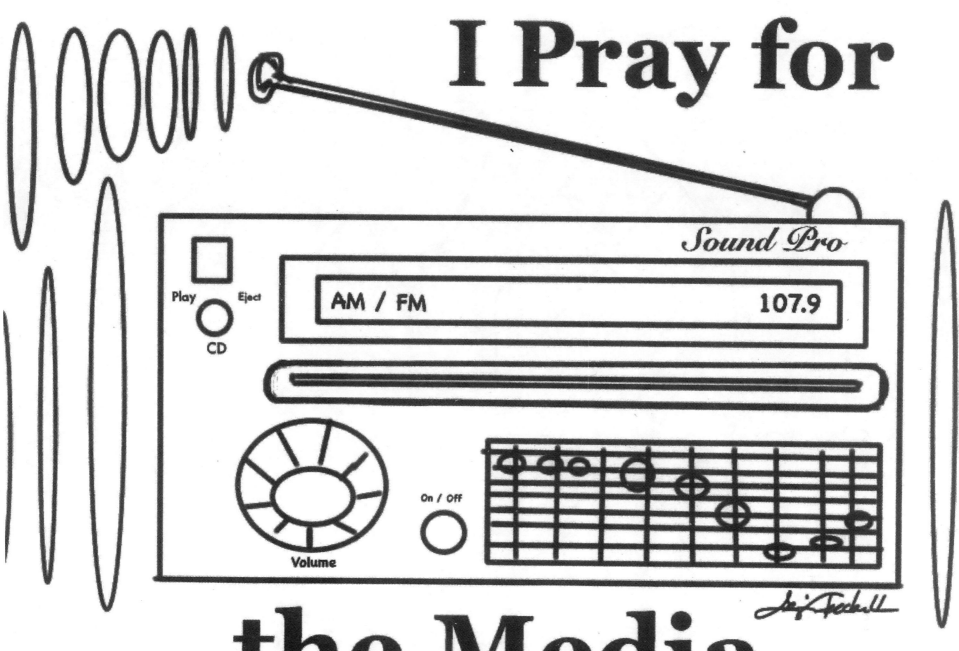

I Pray for the children around the World